TOBACCO IN SONG AND STORY

Published @ 2017 Trieste Publishing Pty Ltd

ISBN 9780649722204

Tobacco in Song and Story by John Bain, Jr.

Edited by Trieste Publishing Pty Ltd.
Cover @ 2017

www.triestepublishing.com

JOHN BAIN, JR.

TOBACCO IN
SONG AND STORY

Trieste

TOBACCO
IN 🌿 🌿 🌿 🌿
SONG AND STORY

COMPILED BY

JOHN BAIN, Jr.

" *It may be weeds I've gathered, too :*
But even weeds may be as fragrant
As the fairest flower with some
Sweet memory."

NEW YORK

ARTHUR GRAY & CO.
1896

COPYRIGHT, 1896,
BY
ARTHUR GRAY.

THE MERSHON COMPANY PRESS,
RAHWAY, N. J.

CONTENTS.

———

iii

CONTENTS. V

INTRODUCTION.

A GOOD book needs no eloquent pen to etch its merits in the way of an introduction.

It was evident, however, to the compiler of this book, that no volume treating on Tobacco had heretofore appeared which contained all that deserved a place in the literature of the weed, and at the same time avoided the scientific treatises and exhaustive histories on the subject which have no interest to the great army of smokers.

This, in brief, is the object of this anthology. All the illustrations in this little volume have been drawn especially for it. The binding and paper are in keeping with the best mechanical features of any book; while its handy size makes of it a book in which any smoker may delight.

There is something in the book that will appeal to every lover of the weed, no matter what his station in life may be or the grade of tobacco he consumes. It is not meant to be any more a book for the smoker of twenty-five cent cigars than for the man behind the clay pipe.

It is intended to be a book of good fellowship, in which all smokers are free and equal.

TOBACCO IN SONG AND STORY.

SIR WALTER RALEIGH.

WALTER RALEIGH'S name will always, among the English-speaking races, be linked with that of Tobacco. Raleigh it was who, in the sixteenth century, found tobacco on the plantations of Virginia, and introduced it into England and Ireland, along with the potato. He planted both upon his estate at Gongall, Ireland, the home presented to him by the auburn-haired, falcon-faced Elizabeth, England's one great queen, for services rendered upon the Spanish Main and in the then New World.

Columbus was the first European to discover tobacco. When he and his companions saw the Indians smoking it and blowing the smoke through their nostrils, they were as much surprised as they had been at the first sight of land. But they were no more surprised than Ben Jonson, Beaumont, Selden, Fletcher, and Shakespeare when, one stormy night, Sir Walter Raleigh walked into the Mermaid tavern and, throwing pipes and tobacco upon the table, invited all hands to smoke. Shakespeare thought that it was anticipating things a little to smoke in this world, and that Bacon should have the monopoly of it; while Ben Jonson— "rare Ben," the roundest and fattest and gruffest of men—after the first pipeful or two, growled: "Tobacco, I do assert, without fear of contradiction from the

Avon skylark, is the most soothing, sovereign, and precious weed that ever our dear old Mother Earth tendered to the use of man! Let him who would contradict that most mild, but sincere and enthusiastic assertion, look to his undertaker. Sir Walter, your health." Then everyone drained his mug's contents, and Sir Walter was happy in the consciousness of having given something to civilized man second only to food.

If the conversation of those master minds that night could have been preserved, few books that we know would equal in wisdom, wit, humor, and brilliancy, a volume made of it. But, alas! there was no Boswell there, with his notebook, his prying eyes and eager ears, and that night has passed into the great sea of oblivion, like the snow that fell, the winds that blew, the flowers that budded, blossomed, faded, withered, and died, three thousand years ago—or thirty.

Something about Sir Walter Raleigh

should here be told, not for the first time,
—nothing nowadays is ever told for the
first time,—but in our own way. A few
pages will epitomize the life of this bold,
handsome, gallant, honest and honorable,
tender and loyal, simple and courage-
ous, sixteenth-century gentleman. None
braver ever lived, loved, sang, suffered,
and died, the best he knew how, than this
jewel of a man. No more romantic life
has been chronicled than his.

He was born in the same year with
Edmund Spenser, 1552; and twelve years
before Kit Marlowe and the glorious
Shakespeare, both of whom came into the
world in 1564. In all the annals of literature, or in all the illimitable worlds of
illimitable space, in all the illimitable ages,
was there ever, or will there ever be such
a quartette gathered under one roof, in
one room (the Mermaid's) as that one
composed of Raleigh, Spenser, Marlowe,
and Shakespeare.

It was at the Hayes Farm, in Devonshire, that Raleigh first saw the light of day. He grew up in the country, from babyhood to his teens, and into them, as other boys do. He loved outdoors, play, study. He was as adventurous as Clive who, later on, gave England India; but unlike Clive, he had his poetic days and nights. Clive was all adventure, boldness, recklessness, and business; Raleigh was all these—except the latter. Moreover, he was a student and a lover of poetry.

Raleigh was educated at Oxford, and, at the age of seventeen, when most English boys are going home for the holidays, roast goose and apple sauce, plum pudding and 'alf-an'-'alf, he began his meteor-like career, as a volunteer in the cause of the French Protestants. For more than five years he fought in the Continental wars, and at the age of twenty-four he joined his half-brother, Sir Humphrey Gilbert, in a voyage to North America. In 1578, two years

later, at the age of twenty-six, he returned to England, with a lot of—Experience. He couldn't make much of a
splurge on that, so we find him, as Captain Raleigh, a little later on, in Ireland,
fighting like a bulldog against the rebel
Desmonds. He fought so well that he was
chosen to bear dispatches from the Lord
Lieutenant of Ireland to Auburn Lizzie.

Fortune's wheel swung round, until
Raleigh stood on top of it the day he
met Elizabeth. She could make or
break any man in England in those days.
Raleigh's star was in her happiest
mood that day when she sent her gallant
protégé up a certain thoroughfare, down
which the bejeweled queen was coming,
for as Lizzie paused at a particularly
muddy place with a shudder of disgust,
young Captain Raleigh whipped off his
cloak and flung it beneath her virgin feet.
She repaid him with a smile, and from
that moment Captain Raleigh was in the
saddle.

In less than no time he was a knight,
Captain of the Queen's Guard, and Sen-
eschal of Cornwall; besides receiving a
grant of twelve thousand acres of land in
Ireland, and the sole right of licensing
wine-sellers in England.

Elizabeth knew how to reward those
in whom she took a platonic interest.
She gave them something besides shawls,
portraits of her effulgent self, and grand-
motherly advice. There was no squatty
royalty about Elizabeth of England.
Nothing was too good for those who
served the state; nothing too severe for
the state's enemies.

Raleigh now had all kinds of money:
money to burn, to throw away, to treat,
spend, and loan. He had a lot of
stranded friends among the poets and
dramatists of that day, and he helped
them all out of his large purse and larger
nature.

Then he lost more than half his fortune
in an attempt to colonize North America.

Twice he sent out expeditions to America, but the ancestors of King Philip and Massasoit would not allow him to do it. The first settlers escaped in their nightcaps and slippers, and boarded Francis Drake's ships; but the second band were tomahawked and scalped. The first expedition brought to England tobacco, and the succulent and necessary Murphy. Raleigh called a State Virginia, after his Virgin Queen, and the capital of North Carolina is known to this day as Raleigh.

In the splendid fight of English seamen against the Armada of Spain—a fleet Philip sent out to wipe England off the map—Raleigh was a leader. Such men as Francis Drake, John Hawkins, and Frobisher were his companions in that never-to-be-forgotten Homeric sea conflict. Then Raleigh became the owner of the magnificent acres of Sherborne, in Dorsetshire; then the disgraced husband of Elizabeth Throgmorton; the daring explorer of the Orinoco ; the hero of the siege of Cadiz and the capture of Fayal; and then Elizabeth died, and James the First, with his big head, slobbering mouth, codfish eyes, spindle shanks, his want of dignity, his drunkenness, his affectation of learning, and his rank cowardice, came to the throne. He had hardly filled the chair left vacant by Elizabeth before Raleigh's star began to sputter like a midnight candle, and Cecil, his former chum, began to poison the king's mind against him. Cecil did his backcapping work so thoroughly, in 1603, when Raleigh was fifty-one years of age, that James had the former favorite stripped of nearly all his honors and rewards.

The world is always full of Cecils, Jameses, and (comparative) Raleighs.

Every man who reads this, knows that.

But worse followed, thanks to the reptile Cecil : Raleigh was charged with

having been at the head of a plot to
kidnap James and place Lady Arabella
Stuart on the throne. He was tried for
treason, in Winchester Castle. He was
sent to the Tower, and for thirteen years
kept there. During those thirteen years,
his friend, William Shakespeare, was becoming the Miracle of Time—the greatest
man ever cast by the tides of Time on
the shores of Life. What a world of
pities that for those thirteen golden years
to Shakespeare, Raleigh never saw one of
the great plays of England's King of
Kings, and that, in 1616, the year Raleigh was released from the Tower to
find gold in America for James the First,
Shakespeare should die! Well, two years
later, Raleigh followed him. But Shakespeare died in bed.

While in the Tower, Raleigh wrote his
" History of the World "; and there he
spent much of his time in chemical ex-
periments, in the course of which he
sought eagerly for the philosopher's

stone, and the elixir of life. But he found them not. They are still with Keely's motor, in the womb of Time.

In 1616, James the First sent Raleigh with fourteen ships to the Orinoco after the tons of gold he thought were there. All Raleigh found was a bar or two of gold, captured from a Spanish settlement on the Orinoco River. His son Walter was killed in the assault upon the settlement, and, " with my brains broken," he wrote his wife, he was forced to sail for home from the grave of his son.

It would be of historic interest to have the grave of young Walter Raleigh located, by the way. Like Ophelia's body, the body of a Raleigh should enrich the soil that has received it.

The Spaniards were wild with rage at Raleigh's acts, and Spain went yelling, into James's audience chamber, " Pirates ! Pirates ! "

Spain demanded reparation. James desired to please Spain, as he wished to

marry his son Charles to the Infanta.
So he had Raleigh arrested on his return
to England, and on October 19, 1618, at
the age of sixty-six, he was beheaded, at
Westminster, upon the fifteen-year-old
charge of " treason." Because a " king "
had committed it, it wasn't called " murder "; but when Cromwell cut off the
head of Charles the First—Horrors !—
that was " murder "—to kill a worthless
" king "; but that was " execution " to
kill a fine gentleman like Raleigh, who
was worth fifty thousand kings by divine
rot.

No man could die more splendidly
than did Raleigh. He smilingly picked
up the axe on his way to the block and,
running his finger over the edge of it,
said :

" This is a sharp medicine, but it will
cure all disease." Two blows, and a
master of the sword, the compass, and
the pen was without a head.

What a pity, that he couldn't have had

a box of perfectos the night before he
left the world ! Well, maybe James the
First, his murderer, is compelled to
smoke " two for five " where he is.

THE DISCOVERY OF TOBACCO.

A Sailor's Version.

THEY were three jolly sailors bold,
  Who sailed across the sea ;
They'd braved the storm, and stood the gale,
  And got to Virgin-ee.

'Twas in the days of good Queen Bess,—
  Or p'raps a bit before,—
And now these here three sailors bold
  Went cruising on the shore.
A lurch to starboard, one to port,
  Now forrard, boys, go we,
With a haul and a "Ho!" and a "That's your
    sort!"
  To find out Tobac-kee.

Says Jack, "This here's a rummy land."
  Says Tom, "Well, shiver me!
The sun shines out as precious hot
  As ever I did see."
Says Dick, "Messmates, since here we be "—
  And gave his eye a wink—
"We've come to find out Tobac-kee,
  Which means a drop to drink."

Says Jack, says he, "The Injins think——"
  Says Tom, "I'll swear as they
Don't think at all." Says Dick, " You're right ;
  It aint their nat'ral way.

But I want to find out, my lads,
  This stuff of which they tell ;
For if, as it aint meant to drink,
  Why, it must be meant to smell."

Says Tom, says he, " To drink or smell,
  I don't think this here's meant."
Says Jack, says he, " Blame my old eyes,
  If I'll believe it's scent."
" Well, then," says Dick, " if that aint square,
  It must be meant for meat ;
So come along, my jovial mates,
  To find what's good to eat."

They came across a great big plant,
  A-growing tall and true.
Says Jack, says he, " I'm precious dry,"
  And picked a leaf to chew.
While Tom takes up a sun-dried bit,
  A-lying by the trees ;
He rubs it in his hands to dust
  And then begins to sneeze.

Another leaf picks nimble Dick,
  And dries it in the sun,
And rolls it up all neat and tight.
  "My lads," said he in fun,
"I mean to cook this precious weed."
  And then from out his poke
With burning-glass he lights the end,
  And quick blows up the smoke.

Says Jack, says he, " Of Paradise
  I've heerd some people tell,"

Says Tom, says he, " This here will do ;
  Let's have another smell."
Says Dick, his face all pleasant smiles,
  A-looking through a cloud,
" It strikes me here's the Cap'n bold,
  And now we'll all be rowed."

Up comes brave Hawkins on the beach ;
  "Shiver my hull!" he cries,
" What's these here games, my merry men?"
  And then, "Why, blame my eyes!
Here's one as chaws, and one as snuffs,
  And t'other of the three
Is smoking like a chimbley-pot—
  They've found out Tobac-kee!"

So if ever you should hear
  Of Raleigh and them lies
About his sarvant and his pipe
  And him as " Fire!" cries,
You say as 'twas three sailors bold
  As sailed to Virgin-ee
In brave old Hawkins' gallant ship
  Who found out Tobac-kee.
          —Cigar and Tobacco World, London.

A FEW WORDS ABOUT TOBACCO.

ALTHOUGH Jean Nicot, a French ambassador to Portugal, is credited with the greatest service in giving tobacco its official recognition, it was really first introduced into Europe in 1558 by Francisco Fernandes, a physician who had been sent by Philip II. of Spain to investigate the products of Mexico.

Nicot, however, on his return to France in about 1560, carried it to Catherine de Medici, the Queen ; and the reception it met with from her and other titled personages gave it reputation and popularity.

From Nicot and the Queen were derived the titles, " Queen's Heat " (*Nicotiana*), and subsequently to one of its preparations, "The Powder of the Queen."

Lofty example and the sanction of high life gave currency to any custom ; hence tobacco became generally used.

The French give Sir Francis Drake the credit of carrying it to England, and there is no doubt but what Sir Walter and Sir Francis succeeded in making tobacco a fashionable luxury. From there it spread. Every lover of the plant can easily imagine the rest.

THE ORIGIN OF TOBACCO.

THE Prophet was taking a stroll in the country when he saw a serpent, stiff with cold, lying on the ground. He compassionately took it up and warmed it in his bosom. When the serpent had recovered, it said :

"Divine Prophet, listen. I am now going to bite thee."

"Why, pray?" inquired Mahomet.

"Because thy race persecutest mine and tries to stamp it out."

"But does not thy race, too, make perpetual war against mine?" was the Prophet's rejoinder. "How canst thou, besides, be so ungrateful, and so soon forget that I saved thy life?"

"There is no such thing as gratitude upon this earth," replied the serpent, "and if I were now to spare thee, either thou or another of thy race would kill me. By Allah, I shall bite thee!"

"If thou hast sworn by Allah, I will not cause thee to break thy vow," said the Prophet, holding his hand to the serpent's mouth. The serpent bit him, but he sucked the wound with his lips and spat the venom on the ground. And on that very spot there sprung up a plant which combines within itself the venom of the serpent and the compassion of the Prophet. Men call this plant by the name of tobacco.—*Conte Arabe.*

CLOUDS.

MORTALS say their hearts are light
  When the clouds around disperse ;
Clouds to gather thick as night,
  Is the smoker's universe.
    —*From the German of Bauernfeld.*

THE SMOKING PHILOSOPHER.

HIS whole amusement was his pipe; and, as there is a certain indefinable link between smoking and philosophy, my father, by dint of smoking, had become a philosopher. It is no less strange than true that we can puff away our cares with tobacco, when without it they remain an oppressive burthen to existence. There is no composing draught like the draught through the tube of a pipe. The savage warriors of North America enjoyed the blessing before we did; and to the pipe is to be ascribed the wisdom of their councils, and the laconic delivery of their sentiments. It would be well introduced into our own legislative assembly. Ladies, indeed, would no longer peep down through the ventilator; but we should have more sense and fewer words. It is also to tobacco that is to be ascribed the stoical firmness of those American warriors who, satisfied with the pipe in their mouths, submitted with perfect indifference to the torture of their enemies. From the virtues of this weed arose that peculiar expression when you irritate another, that you " put his pipe out."

—Marryat's " Jacob Faithful."

WITH PIPE AND BOOK.

WITH Pipe and Book at close of day,
Oh, what is sweeter, mortal, say ?
It matters not what book on knee,
Old Izaak or the Odyssey,
It matters not meerschaum or clay.

And though one's eyes will dream astray,
And lips forget to sue or sway,
It is "enough to merely be "
   With Pipe and Book.

What though our modern skies be gray,
As bards aver, I will not pray
For "soothing Death " to succor me,
But ask this much, O Fate, of thee,
A little longer yet to stay
   With Pipe and Book.
          —RICHARD LE GALLIENNE.

CARLYLE ON TOBACCO.

"Tobacco smoke," says Carlyle, "is the one element in which, by our European manners, men can sit silent together without embarrassment, and where no man is bound to speak one word more than he has actually and veritably got to say. Nay, rather every man is admonished and enjoined by the laws of honor, and even of personal ease, to stop short of that point; and at all events to hold his peace and take to his pipe again the instant he *has* spoken his meaning, if he chance to have any. The results of which salutary practice, if introduced into constitutional parliaments, might evidently be incalculable. The essence of what little intellect and insight there is in that room—we shall or can get nothing more out of any parliament; and sedative, gently soothing, gently clarifying, tobacco smoke (if the room were well ventilated,

open atop, and the air kept good), with
the obligation to a *minimum* of speech,
surely gives human intellect and insight
the best chance they can have."

IN FAVOR OF TOBACCO.

MUCH victuals serves for gluttony
To fatten men like swine ;
But he's a frugal man indeed
That with a leaf can dine,
And needs no napkin for his hands,
His fingers' ends to wipe,
But keeps his kitchen in a box,
And roast meat in a pipe.
      —SAMUEL ROWLANDS.
           Knave of Clubs (1611).

A PIPE OF TOBACCO.

LITTLE tube of mighty power,
Charmer of an idle hour,
Object of my warm desire,
Lip of wax, and eye of fire :
And thy snowy taper waist,
With my finger gently braced ;
And thy pretty swelling crest,
With my little stopper press'd,
And the sweetest bliss of blisses,
Breathing from thy balmy kisses.

Happy thrice, and thrice agen,
Happiest he of happy men,
Who when agen the night returns,
When agen the taper burns;
When agen the cricket's gay
(Little cricket full of play),
Can afford his tube to feed
With the fragrant Indian weed;
Pleasure for a nose divine,
Incense of the god of wine.
Happy thrice, and thrice agen
Happiest he of happy men.
              —ISAAC HAWKINS BROWNE (1736).

BULWER-LYTTON ON TOBACCO SMOKING.

HE who doth not smoke hath either known no great griefs, or refuseth himself the softest consolation, next to that which comes from heaven. "What softer than a woman?" whispers the young reader.

Young reader, woman teases as well as consoles. Woman makes half the sorrows which she boasts the privilege to soothe.

Woman consoles us, it is true, while we are young and handsome; when we are old and ugly, woman snubs and scolds us.

On the whole, then, woman in this scale, the weed in that. Jupiter! hang out thy balance, and weigh them both; and if thou give the preference to woman, all I can say is, the next time Juno ruffles thee, O Jupiter! try the weed.—"*What Will He Do with It?*"

INVOCATION TO TOBACCO.

WEED of the strange flower, weed of the earth,
Killer of dullness, parent of mirth,
Come in the sad hour, come in the gay,
Appear in the night, or in the day,—
Still thou art welcome as June's blooming rose,
Joy of the palate, delight of the nose!

Weed of the green field, weed of the wild,
Fostered in freedom, America's child,
Come in Virginia, come in Havana;
Friend of the universe, sweeter than manna—
Still thou art welcome, rich, fragrant, and ripe,
Pride of the tube-case, delight of the pipe!

Weed of the savage, weed of each pole,
Comforting, soothing philosophy's soul,

Come in the snuff-box, come in cigar,
In Strasburgh and Kings', come from afar,—
Still thou art welcome, the purest, the best,
Joy of earth's millions, forever caresst !
                    —HENRY JAMES MELLEN.

THE HAPPY SMOKER.

WHEN I am "broke," I take a smoke—
        Comfort is my aim—
Likewise when "flush"—or maybe "lush,"
        I gently nurse the flame.
The wreaths of smoke that round me roll,
From "Garcia" or from carven bowl,
        Drive care away
        And make the day—
If dark, all bright ; if bright, then more
Of joy is added to my store.
And so I puff, morn, noon, and night,
The gods be thanked for this sweet "light."
                    —E. BONFILS.

SAM SLICK ON THE VIRTUES OF A PIPE.

"THE fact is, squire, the moment a man takes to a pipe, he becomes a philosopher. It's the poor man's friend; it calms the mind, soothes the temper, and makes a man patient under difficulties. It has made more good men, good husbands, kind masters, indulgent fathers, than any other blessed thing on this universal earth."

—" *Sam Slick, the Clockmaker.*"

OPINION OF ST. PIERRE ON THE EFFECT OF TOBACCO.

THE author of "Paul and Virginia" remarks : " It is true that tobacco in some measure augments our power of judgment by exciting the nerves of the brain. This plant is, however, a veritable poison, and in the long run affects the sense of smell and sometimes the nerves of the eye. But man is always ready to impair his physical constitution provided he can strengthen his 'intellectual sentiment' thereby."

SMOKE DREAMS.

TOBACCO smoke! Blue-gray in wreaths,—
  Blue laurel-wreaths which float in air,
As if, invisible, serene,
  A dreaming angel hovered there.
A spirit of calm kindliness,—
  A touch of eyes that smile through tears,—
A mantle of forgetfulness,
  Thrown on the passions of the years.

I cross my knees, I puff my pipe,
  The gentle Summer warmth creeps in ;
The Summer warmth 'mid Winter's snows,—
  For indolence shall banish sin,—
And watch the tasseled smoke-drops fall,
  And note the fringed smoke-plumes rise,
And see the dreams, in legions, turn
  To smoky nothings in the skies.

Tobacco smoke, like silken web,
  Suspended in the restful airs,
To me and mine, in soothing rhymes
  A dainty, artless burden bears ;
Let cares rage on—let hopes renew—
  The Yesterday, To-morrow be—
But we are wise, the smoke and I ;
  We cease regrets and troubles flee.
                              —A. B. TUCKER.

GUIZOT.

A LADY, one evening, calling on Guizot, the historian of France, found him absorbed in his pipe.   In astonishment she exclaimed : " What ! you smoke and yet have arrived at so great an age ! "   " Ah, madam," replied the venerable statesman, "if I had not smoked I should have been dead ten years ago."

MY PIPE.

WHEN love grows cool, thy fire still warms me ;
When friends are fled, thy presence charms me.
If thou art full, though purse be bare,
I smoke and cast away all care !
—*German Smoking Song.*

LATAKIA.

WHEN all the panes are hung with frost,
  Wild wizard-work of silver lace,
I draw my sofa on the rug,
  Before the ancient chimney-place.
Upon the painted tiles are mosques
  And minarets, and here and there
A blind muezzin lifts his hands,
  And calls the faithful unto prayer.
Folded in idle, twilight dreams,
I hear the hemlock chirp and sing,
As if within its ruddy core
It held the happy heart of spring.
Ferdousi never sang like that,
  Nor Saadi grave, nor Hafiz gay ;
I lounge, and blow white rings of smoke,
  And watch them rise and float away.

The curling wreaths like turbans seem
  Of silent slaves that come and go—
Or Viziers, packed with craft and crime,
Whom I behead from time to time,
  With pipe-stem, at a single blow.
And now and then a lingering cloud
  Takes gracious form at my desire,
And at my side my lady stands,
Unwinds her veil with snowy hands—
  A shadowy shape, a breath of fire !
Oh, Love ! if you were only here,
  Beside me in this mellow light,

Though all the bitter winds should blow,
And all the ways be choked with snow ;
'Twould be a true Arabian night!
                    —T. B. ALDRICH.

SUBLIME TOBACCO.

SUBLIME tobacco! which, from east to west,
Cheers the tar's labor or the Turkman's rest ;
Which on the Moslem's ottoman divides
His hours, and rivals opium and his brides ;
Magnificent in Stamboul, but less grand,
Though not less loved, in Wapping on the
          Strand ;
Divine in hookas, glorious in a pipe,
When tipp'd with amber, mellow, rich, and
          ripe ;
Like other charmers, wooing the caress
More dazzlingly when daring in full dress ;
Yet thy true lovers more admire, by far,
Thy naked beauties—give me a cigar!
                    —LORD BYRON,
          The Island, Canto ii, Stanza 19.

VIRGINIA TOBACCO.

Two maiden dames of sixty-two
  Together long had dwelt;
Neither, alas! of love so true
  The bitter pang had felt.

But age comes on, they say, apace,
  To warn us of our death,
And wrinkles mar the fairest face,—
  At last it stops our breath.

One of these dames, tormented sore
  With that curst pang, toothache,
Was at a loss for such a bore
  What remedy to take.

"I've heard," thought she, "this ill to cure,
  A pipe is good, they say.
Well, then, tobacco I'll endure,
  And smoke the pain away."

The pipe was lit, the tooth soon well,
  And she retired to rest,
When then the other ancient belle
  Her spinster maid addressed,—

"Let me request a favor, pray"—
  "I'll do it if I can"—
"Oh! well, then, love, smoke every day,
  You smell so like a man! "
                    —JOHN STANLEY GREGSON.

A GOOD CIGAR.

OH, 'tis well enough
A whiff or a puff
  From the heart of a pipe to get;
And a dainty maid
Or a budding blade
  May toy with the cigarette;
But a man, when the time
Of a glorious prime
  Dawns forth like a morning star,
Wants the dark-brown bloom
And the sweet perfume
  That go with a good cigar.

To lazily float
In a painted boat
  On a shimmering morning sea,
Or to flirt with a maid,
In the afternoon shade,
  Seems good enough sport to be;
But the evening hour,
With its subtle power,
  Is sweeter and better far,
If joined to the joy,
Devoid of alloy,
  That lurks in a good cigar.

When a blanket wet
Is solidly set
  O'er hopes prematurely grown;

When ambition is tame,
And energy lame,
    And the bloom from the fruit is blown;
When to dance and to dine,
With women and wine,
    Past poverty pleasures are,—
A man's not bereft
Of all peace, if there's left
    The joy of a good cigar.
                          —NORRIS BULL.

A POET'S PIPE.

From the French of Charles Baudelaire.

A POET'S pipe am I,
And my Abyssinian tint
Is an unmistakable hint
That he lays me not often by.
When his soul is with grief o'erworn,
I smoke like the cottage where
They are cooking the evening fare
For the laborer's return.

I enfold and cradle his soul
In the vapors moving and blue
That mount from my fiery mouth;
And there is power in my bowl
To charm his spirit and soothe,
And heal his weariness too.
                —RICHARD HERNE SHEPHERD.

THE HAPPY SMOKING GROUND.

WHEN that last pipe is smoked at last
  And pouch and pipe put by,
And smoked and smoker both alike
  In dust and ashes lie,
What of the smoker? Whither passed?
  Ah, will he smoke no more?
And will there be no golden cloud
  Upon the golden shore?
Ah! who shall say we cry in vain
  To fate upon his hill,
For, howsoe'er we ask and ask,
  · He goes on smoking still.
But, surely, 'twere a bitter thing
  If other men pursue
Their various earthly joys again
  Beyond that distant blue,
If the poor smoker might not ply
  His peaceful passion too.
If Indian braves may still up there
  On merry scalpings go,
And buried Britons rise again
  With arrow and with bow,
May not the smoker hope to take
  His "cutty" from below?
So let us trust! and when at length
  You lay me 'neath the yew,
Forget not, O my friends, I pray,
  Pipes and tobacco too!
                —RICHARD LE GALLIENNE.

A FAREWELL TO TOBACCO.

MAY the Babylonish curse
Straight confound my stammering verse
If I can a passage see
In this word-perplexity,
Or a fit expression find,
Or a language to my mind
(Still the phrase is wide or scant)
To take leave of thee, Great Plant!
Or in any terms relate
Half my love or half my hate :
For I hate yet love thee so,
That, whichever things I show,
The plain truth will seem to be
A constrain'd hyperbole,
And the passion to proceed
More from a mistress than a weed.

Sooty retainer to the vine
Bacchus' black servant, negro-fine ;
Sorcerer, thou makest us dote upon
Thy begrimed complexion,
And for thy pernicious sake,
More and greater oaths to break
Than reclaimèd lovers take
'Gainst women ; thou thy siege dost lay
Much too in the female way,
While thou suck'st the laboring breath
Faster than kisses or than death.

Thou in such a cloud dost bind us
That our worst foes cannot find us,
And ill fortune, that would thwart us,
Shoots at rovers, shooting at us ;
While each man, through thy height'ning
    steam
Does like a smoking Etna seem,
And all about us does express
(Fancy and wit in richest dress)
A Sicilian fruitfulness.

Thou through such a mist dost show us
That our best friends do not know us,
And for those allowèd features,
Due to reasonable creatures,
Liken'st us to fell Chimeras—
Monsters that, who see us, fear us ;
Worse than Cerberus or Geryon
Or, who first loved a cloud, Ixion.

Bacchus we know, and we allow
His tipsy rites.   But what art thou,
That but by reflex canst show
What his deity can do,
As the false Egyptian spell
Aped the true Hebrew miracle,
Some few vapors thou may'st raise,
The weak brain may serve to amaze,
But to the reins and nobler heart
Canst not life nor heat impart.

Brother of Bacchus, later born,
The old world was sure forlorn

Wanting thee; thou aidest more
The god's victories than before
All his panthers and the brawls
Of his piping Bacchanals.
These as stale, we disallow,
Or judge of *thee* meant: only thou
His true Indian conquest art;
And, for ivy round his dart,
The reformèd god now weaves
A finer thyrsus of thy leaves.

Scent to match thy rich perfume
Through his quaint alembic strain,
None so sovereign to the brain.
Nature that did in thee excel,
Framed again no second smell.
Roses, violets but toys
For the smaller sort of boys,
Or for greener damsels meant;
Thou art the only manly scent.

Stinking'st of the stinking kind,
Filth of the mouth and fogs of the mind;
Africa, that brags her foison,
Breeds no such prodigious poison,
Henbane, nightshade, both together,
Hemlock, aconite—
                    Nay, rather,
Plant divine, of rarest virtue;
Blisters on the tongue would hurt you.
'Twas but in a sort I blamed thee,
None e'er prosper'd who defamed thee:
Irony all and feign'd abuse,
Such as perplexed lovers use

At a need when, in despair,
To paint forth their fairest fair,
Or in part but to express
That exceeding comeliness
Which their fancies doth so strike,
They borrow language of dislike,
And, instead of Dearest Miss,
Jewel, Honey, Sweetheart, Bliss,
Call her Cockatrice and Siren,
Basilisk, and all that's evil,
Witch, Hyena, Mermaid, Devil,
Ethiop, Wench, and Blackamoor,
Monkey, Ape, and twenty more:
Friendly Traitress, Loving Foe—
Not that she is truly so,
But no other way they know
A contentment to express,
Borders so upon excess,
That they do not rightly wot
Whether it be pain or not.

Or as men, constrain'd to part
With what's nearest to their heart,
While their sorrow's at the height,
Lose discrimination quite,
And their hasty wrath let fall
To appease their frantic gall,
On the darling thing whatever
Whence they feel it death to sever,
Though it be, as they, perforce,
Guiltless of the sad divorce.
For I must (nor let it grieve thee,
Friendliest of plants, that I must) leave
   thee.

For thy sake, Tobacco, I
Would do anything but die,
And but seek to extend my days
Long enough to sing thy praise.

But as she who once hath been
A king's consort is a queen
Ever after, nor will bate
Any tittle of her state
Though a widow, or divorced,
So I from my converse forced,
The old name and style retain,
A right Katherine of Spain ;
And a seat, too, 'mongst the joys
Of the blest Tobacco Boys ;
Where, though I, by sour physician,
Am debarr'd the full fruition
Of thy favors, I may catch
Some collateral sweets, and snatch
Sidelong odors, that give life
Like glances from a neighbor's wife ;
And still live in the by-places
And the suburbs of thy graces,
And in thy borders take delight
An unconquer'd Canaanite.
—CHARLES LAMB.

INSCRIPTION FOR A TOBACCO JAR.

KEEP me at hand ; and as my fumes arise,
You'll find a *jar* the gates of Paradise.
—*Cope's Tobacco Plant.*

THE SCENT OF A GOOD CIGAR.

WHAT is it comes through the deepening
  dusk,—
  Something sweeter than jasmine scent,
  Sweeter than rose and violet blent,
More potent in power than orange or musk?
    The scent of a good cigar.

I am all alone in my quiet room,
  And the windows are open wide and free
  To let in the south wind's kiss for me,
While I rock in the softly gathering gloom,
    And that subtle fragrance steals.

Just as a loving, tender hand
  Will sometimes steal in yours,
  It softly comes through the open doors,
And memory wakes at its command,—
    The scent of that good cigar.

And what does it say? Ah! that's for me
  And my heart alone to know ;
  But that heart thrills with a sudden glow,
Tears fill my eyes till I cannot see,—
    From the scent of that good cigar.
            —KATE A. CARRINGTON.

IN THE OL' TOBACKER PATCH.

I JESS kind o' feel so lonesome that I don't know
    what to do,
    When I think about them days we used to
    spend
A-hoein' our tobacker in th' clearin'—me an'
    you—
    An' a-wishin' that the day was at an end.
For the dewdrops was a-sparklin' on the
    beeches' tender leaves
    As we started out a-workin' in the morn;
An' th' noonday sun was sendin' down a shower
    of burnin' leaves
    When we heard the welcome-soundin' dinner-
    horn.
An' th' shadders round us gathered in a sort of
    ghostly batch,
'Fore we started home from workin' in that
    ol' tobacker patch.

I'm a-feelin' mighty lonesome, as I look aroun'
    to-day,
    For I see th' change that's taken place since
    then.
All th' hills is brown and faded, for th' woods
    is cleared away,
    You an' me has changed from ragged boys
    to men;

You are livin' in th' city that we ust to dream
    about ;
  I am still a-dwellin' here upon the place,
But my form is bent an' feeble, which was once
    so straight and stout,
  An' there's most a thousand wrinkles on my
    face.
You have made a mint of money ; I perhaps
    have been your match,
But we both enjoyed life better in that ol'
    tobacker patch.
                —S. Q. LAPIUS.

MOTTO FOR A TOBACCO JAR.

COME! don't refuse sweet Nicotina's aid,
But woo the goddess through a yard of clay ;
And soon you'll own she is the fairest maid
To stifle pain, and drive old Care away.
Nor deem it waste, what though to ash she
    burns,
If for your outlay you get good returns !

A STUB OF CIGAR.

YOU ask what it means, and a look of scorn
  Mars your fair face, dear Lady Disdain ;
But to me it recalls a bright summer morn
  When cherries were red down a long country
    lane !

I close my eyes, and a rustle of wheat
  Comes borne on a breeze whose breath is a
    balm ;
A breeze heavy with sweet clover-bloom at my
    feet,
  Which brings to my spirit an infinite calm.

And once more I see, though my eyes are
    closed fast,
  A face kindly tender, and manly, and true—
A friendship once vowed that was given to
    last,
  And eyes that reflected the heaven's own
    blue.

As two sailing ships in mid-ocean meet,
  Salute, and pass on to far distant lands,
We met, to find only friendship was sweet,
  When we were compelled to clasp parting
    hands.

And the voice of that comrade who strolled by
    my side
  Comes again to my ear, thro' days vanished
    afar,
And that's why I cherish it, almost with pride,
  This poor, little, wasted, sad stub of cigar !
                    —VOLNEY STREAMER.

  July 2, 1889.

THE PIPE YOU MAKE YOUR-SELF.

THERE'S clay pipes an' briar pipes and meerschaum pipes as well ;
There's plain pipes an' fancy pipes—things jest
   made to sell ;
But any pipe that can be bought fer marbles,
   chalk, or pelf,
Aint ekal to the flaver of the pipe you make
   yourself.

Jest take a common corn cob an' whittle out
   the middle,
Then plug up one end of it as tight as any
   fiddle ;
Fit a stem into th' side an' lay her on th' shelf,
An' when she's dry you take her down—that
   pipe you made yourself.

Cram her full clar to th' brim with nachral
   leaf, you bet—
'Twill smoke a trifle better for bein' somewhat
   wet—
Take your worms and fishin' pole, and a jug
   along for health ;
An' you'll get a taste o' heaven from that pipe
   you made yourself.

                        —HENRY E. BROWN.

SMOKING AWAY.

FLOATING away like the fountain's spray,
  Or the snow-white plume of a maiden,
The smoke-wreaths rise to the starlit skies
  With blissful fragrance laden.

Chorus.—Then smoke away till a golden ray
      Lights up the dawn of the morrow,
    For a cheerful cigar, like a shield, will
      bar,
      The blows of care and sorrow.

The leaf burns bright like the gems of night
  That flash in the braids of Beauty ;
It nerves each heart for the hero's part
  On the battle plain of duty.

In the thoughtful gloom of his darkened room,
  Sits the child of song and story,
But his heart is light, for his pipe burns bright,
  And his dreams are all of glory.

By the blazing fire sits the gray-haired sire,
  And infant arms surround him ;
And he smiles on all in that quaint old hall,
  While the smoke-curls float around him.

In the forest grand of our native land,
  When the savage conflict ended,
The " Pipe of Peace " brought a sweet release
  From toil and terror blended.

The dark-eyed train of the maids of Spain,
  Neath their arbor shades trip lightly,
And a gleaming cigar, like a newborn star,
  In the clasp of their lips burns brightly.

It warms the soul, like the blushing bowl,
  With its rose-red burden streaming,
And drowns it in bliss, like the first warm kiss,
  From the lips with love-buds teaming.
                    —FRANCIS MILES FRENCH.

TOBACCO.

THE Indian weed, withered quite,
Green at noon, cut down at night,
Shows thy decay ; all flesh is hay.
Thus thinke, then drinke tobacco.

The pipe that is so lily-white
Shows thee to be a mortal wight ;
And even such, gone with a touch.
Thus thinke, then drinke tobacco.

And when the smoke ascends on high,
Thinke thou beholdst the vanity
Of worldly stuffe, gone with a puffe.
Thus thinke, then drinke tobacco.

And when the pipe grows foul within,
Think on thy soule defil'd with sin,
And then the fire it doth require.
Thus thinke, then drinke tobacco.

The ashes that are left behind
May serve to put thee still in mind,
That unto dust return thou must.
Thus thinke, then drinke tobacco.
            —GEORGE WITHER, 1620.

A MAIDEN'S WISH.

THE following is derived from a New York paper: " A thoughtful girl says that when she dies she desires to have tobacco planted over her grave, that the weed nourished by her dust may be chewed by her bereaved lovers." Steinmetz has suggested the lines given below as a suitable epitaph for this tobacco-loving maiden :

" Let no cold marble o'er my body rise,
But only earth above and sunny skies.
Thus would I lowly lie in peaceful rest,
Nursing the Herb Divine, from out my breast.
Green let it grow above this clay of mine,
Deriving strength from strength that I resign.
So in the days to come, when I'm beyond
This fickle life, will come my lovers fond,
And, gazing on the plant, their grief restrain
In whispering, 'Lo! dear Anna blooms again!' "

MY CIGARETTE.

MY CIGARETTE! The amulet
  That charms afar unrest and sorrow,
The magic wand that, far beyond
  To-day, can conjure up to-morrow.
Like love's desire, thy crown of fire
  So softly with the twilight blending;
And ah! meseems a poet's dreams
Are in thy wreaths of smoke ascending.

My cigarette! Can I forget
  How Kate and I, in sunny weather,
Sat in the shade the elm-tree made
  And rolled the fragrant weed together?
I at her side, beatified,
  To hold and guide her fingers willing;
She rolling slow the paper's snow,
  Putting my heart in with the filling.

My cigarette! I see her yet,
  The white smoke from her red lips curling
Her dreaming eyes, her soft replies,
  Her gentle sighs, her laughter purling;
Ah, dainty roll, whose parting soul
  Ebbs out in many a snowy billow;
I, too, would burn, if I could earn
  Upon her lips, so soft a pillow.

Ah, cigarette! The gay coquette
  Has long forgot the flame she lighted;

And you, as I, unthinking by,
  Alike are thrown, alike are slighted.
The darkness gathers fast without,
  A raindrop on my window plashes;
My cigarette and heart are out,
  And naught is left me but the ashes.
                    —CHARLES F. LUMMIS.

THOSE ASHES.

UP to the frescoed ceiling
  The smoke of my cigarette
In a sinuous spray is reeling,
  Forming flower and minaret.

What delicious landscape floating
  On perfumed wings I see ;
Pale swans I am idly noting,
  And queens robed in filigree.

I see such delicious faces
  As ne'er man saw before,
And my fancy fondly chases
  Sweet maids on a fairy shore.

Now to bits my air-castle crashes,
  And those pictures I see no more;
My grandmother yells : "Them ashes—
  Don't drop them on the floor !"
                    —R. K. MUNKITTRICK.

HOW IT ONCE WAS.

RIGHT stout and strong the worthy burghers
    stood,
        Or rather, sat,
Drank beer in plenty, ate abundant food ;
For they to ancient customs still were true,
And smoked, and smoked, because they surely
    knew
        What they were at.

William the Testy ruled New Amsterdam—
        A tall man he—
Whose rule was meant by him to be no sham,
But rather like the stern parental style
That sways the city now.   He made the while
        A rough decree.

He ordered that the pipes should cease to
    smoke,
        From that day on.
The people took the order as a joke ;
They did not think, who smoked from child-
    hood up,
That one man such delight would seek to stop,
        Even in fun.

But when at last it dawned upon their minds
        That this was meant,
They closed their houses, shut their window-
    blinds.

Brought forth tobacco from their ample hoard,
And to the governor's house with one accord
      The Burghers went.

They carried chairs, and sat without a word
      Before his porch,
And smoked, and smoked, and not a sound was
    heard,
Till Kieft came forth to take the morning air,
With speech that would have burned them
    then and there,
      If words could scorch.

But they, however savagely he spoke,
      Made no reply.
Higher and thicker rose the clouds of smoke,
And Kieft, perceiving that they would be free,
Tried not to put in force his harsh decree ;
      But let it die.
                  —New York Sun.

BEER.

[*By George Arnold, New York, 1862.*]

HERE,
With my beer,
I sit,
While golden moments flit.
Alas!
They pass
Unheeded by:
And as they fly, I,
Being dry,
Sit, idly sipping here
My beer!
Oh, finer far
Than fame or riches are
The graceful smoke wreaths of this free cigar.
Why
Should I
Weep, wail, or sigh?
What if Luck has passed me by?
What if my hopes are dead,
My pleasures fled ;
Have I not still
My fill
Of right good cheer—
Cigars and beer?
Go, whining youth,
Forsooth!
Go, weep and wail,
Sigh and grow pale,

Weave melancholy rhymes
On the old times,
Whose joys, like shadowy ghosts, appear :
But leave to me my beer !
Gold is dross,
Love is loss,
So, if I gulp my sorrows down,
Or see them drown
In foamy draughts of old nut-brown,
Then do I wear the crown,
Without the cross !

———

SIR WALTER RALEIGH ! name of worth,
   How sweet for thee to know
King James, who never smoked on earth,
   Is smoking down below.

———

ON A TOBACCO JAR.

THREE hundred years ago or soe,
One worthy knight and gentlemanne
Did bring me here, to charm and chere,
To physical and mental manne.
God bless his soule who filled ye bowle,
And may our blessings find him !
That he not miss some share of blisse
Who left soe much behind him.
                    —BERNARD BARKER.

'TWAS OFF THE BLUE CANARIES.

'TWAS off the blue Canary Isles,
  A glorious summer day,
I sat upon the quarter-deck,
  And whiffed my cares away ;
And as the volumed smoke arose,
  Like incense in the air,
I breathed a sigh to think, in sooth,
  It was my last cigar.

I leaned upon the quarter rail,
  And looked down in the sea ;
E'en there the purple wreath of smoke
  Was curling gracefully ;
Oh ! what had I at such a time
  To do with wasting care?
Alas ! the trembling tear proclaimed
  It was my last cigar.

I watched the ashes as it came
  Fast drawing to an end ;
I watched it as a friend would watch
  Beside a dying friend ;
But still the flame swept slowly on ;
  It vanished into air ;
I threw it from me,—spare the tale,—
  It was my last cigar.

I've seen the land of all I love
  Fade in the distance dim;
I've watched above the blighted heart,
  Where once proud hope had been;
But I've never known a sorrow
  That could with that compare,
When off the blue Canaries
  I smoked my last cigar.
            —JOSEPH WARREN FABENS.

IN WREATHS OF SMOKE.

IN wreaths of smoke, blown waywardwise,
Faces of olden days uprise,
  And in his dreamer's reverie
  They haunt the smoker's brain, and he
Breathes for the past regretful sighs.

Mem'ries of maids, with azure eyes,
In dewy dells, 'neath June's soft skies,
Faces that more he'll only see
    In wreaths of smoke.

Eheu, eheu! how fast time flies,—
How youth-time passion droops and dies,
  And all the countless visions flee!
  How worn would all those faces be,
Were not they swathed in soft disguise
    In wreaths of smoke!
            —FRANK NEWTON HOLMAN.

THE OLD CLAY PIPE.

THERE'S a lot of solid comfort
  In an old clay pipe, I find,
If you're kind of out of humor
  Or in trouble in your mind.
When you're feeling awful lonesome
  And don't know just what to do,
There's a heap of satisfaction
  If you smoke a pipe or two.

The ten thousand pleasant memories
  That are buried in your soul
Are playing hide and seek with you
  Around that smoking bowl.
These are mighty restful moments ;
  You're at peace with all the world,
And the panorama changes
  As the thin blue smoke is curled.

Now you cross the bridge of sorrows,
  Now you enter pleasant lands,
And before an open doorway
  You will linger to shake hands
With a lithe and girlish figure
  That is coming through the door ;
Ah ! you recognize the features :
  You have seen that face before.

You are at the dear old homestead
  Where you spent those happy years ;

You are romping with the children ;
  You are smiling through your tears ;
You have fought and whipped the bully—
  You are eight and he is ten.
Oh ! how rapidly we travel—
  You are now a boy again.

You approach the open doorway,
  And before the old armchair
You will stop and kiss the grandma,
  You will smooth the thin white hair ;
You will read the open Bible,
  For the lamp is lit, you see.
It is now your hour for bedtime
  And you kneel at mother's knee.

Still you linger at the hearthstone ;
  You are loath to leave the place ;
When an apple cut's in progress
  You must wait and dance with Grace.
What's the matter with the music ?
  Only this : the pipe is broke,
And a thousand pleasant fancies
  Vanish promptly with the smoke.
                    —A. B. VAN FLEET.

KNICKERBOCKER.

SHADE of Herrick, Muse of Locker,
Help me sing of Knickerbocker !
Boughton, had you bid me chant
Hymns to Peter Stuyvesant,

Had you bid me sing of Wouter,
He, the onion head, the doubter!
But to rhyme of this one—Mocker!
Who shall rhyme to Knickerbocker?
Nay, but where my hand must fail,
There the more shall yours avail;
You shall take your brush and paint
All that ring of figures quaint,—
All those Rip Van Winkle jokers,
All those solid-looking smokers,
Pulling at their pipes of amber,
In the dark-beamed Council Chamber.

Only art like yours can touch
Shapes so dignified—and Dutch;
Only art like yours can show
How the pine logs gleam and glow,
'Till the firelight laughs and passes
'Twixt the tankards and the glasses,
Touching with responsive graces
All those grave Batavian faces,
Making bland and beatific
All that session soporific.

Then I come and write beneath:
Boughton, he deserves the wreath;
He can give us form and hue—
This the Muse can never do!
                    —AUSTIN DOBSON.

ODE TO TOBACCO.

THOU who, when fears attack,
Bidst them avaunt, and black
Care, at the horseman's back
    Perching unseatest ;
Sweet, when the morn is gray ;
Sweet, when they've cleared away
Lunch, at the close of day,
    Possibly sweetest :

I have a liking old
For thee, though manifold
Stories, I know, are told,
    Not to thy credit ;
How one (or two at most)
Drops make a cat a ghost—
Useless, except to roast—
    Doctors have said it :

How they who use fusees
All grow by slow degrees
Brainless as chimpanzees,
    Meager as lizards,
Go mad and beat their wives ;
Plunge (after shocking lives)
Razors and carving knives
    Into their gizzards :

Confound such knavish tricks!
Yet know I five or six
Smokers who freely mix
    Still with their neighbors ;
Jones (who I'm glad to say,
Asked leave of Mrs. J.)
Daily absorbs a clay
    After his labors :

Cats may have had their goose
Cooked by tobacco juice ;
Still why deny its use
    Thoughtfully taken?
We're not as tabbies are :
Smith, take a fresh cigar !
Jones, the tobacco jar !
    Here's to thee, Bacon !
        —C. S. CALVERLEY.

MY FRIENDLY PIPE.

LET sybarites still dream delights
  While smoking cigarettes,
Whose opiates get in their pates,
  Till waking brings regrets ;
Oh, let them doze, devoid of woes,
  Of troubles, and of frets.

And let the chap who loves to nap
  With his cigar in hand

Pursue his way, and live his day,
  As runs Time's changing sand ;
Let him delight, by day and night,
  In his peculiar brand.

But as for me, I love to be
  Provided with a pipe ;
A rare old bowl, to warm my soul,
  A meerschaum, brown and ripe—
Nor good plug cut, no stump or butt,
  Nor filthy gutter snipe.

My joys increase ! It brings me peace,
  As nothing else can do ;
From all the strife of daily life,
  Here my relief is true.
I watch its rings ; it purrs and sings—
  And, then, it's cheaper, too !
                        —*Detroit Tribune.*

CHOOSING A WIFE BY A PIPE OF TOBACCO.

TUBE, I love thee as my life ;
By thee I mean to choose a wife.
Tube, thy *color* let me find,
In her *skin*, and in her *mind*.
Let her have a *shape* as fine ;
Let her breath be sweet as thine ;
Let her, when her lips I kiss,
Burn like thee, to give me bliss ;

Let her in some *smoke* or other,
All my failings kindly smother.
Often when my thoughts are *low*,
Send them where they ought to go ;
When to study I incline,
Let her aid be such as thine ;
Such as thine the charming power
In the vacant social hour.
Let her live to give delight,
Ever *warm* and ever *bright ;*
Let her deeds, whene'er she dies,
Mount as incense to the skies.
—Gentleman's Magazine.

A BACHELOR'S SOLILOQUY.

MY oldest pipe, my dearest girl,
  Alas ! which shall it be ?
For she has said that I must choose
  Betwixt herself and thee.

Farewell, old pipe ; for many years
  You've been my closest friend,
And ever ready at my side
  Thy solace sweet to lend.

No more from out thy weedy bowl,
  When fades the twilight's glow,
Will visions fair and sweet arise
  Or fragrant fancies flow.

No more by flick'ring candlelight
  Thy spirit I'll invoke,

To build my castles in the air
  With wreaths of wav'ring smoke.

And so farewell, a long farewell—
  Until the wedding's o'er,
And then I'll go on smoking thee,
  Just as I did before.
          —EDMUND DAY,
          In the Dramatic Mirror.

———

I LIKE cigars
Beneath the stars,
  Upon the waters blue.
To laugh and float
While rocks the boat
  Upon the waves—don't you?

To rest the oar
And float to shore,—
  While soft the moonbeams shine,—
To laugh and joke
And idly smoke,
  I think is quite divine.
        —ELLA WHEELER WILCOX.

BISMARCK'S LAST CIGAR.

GRANT and Bismarck, the one the European, and the other the American "man of blood and iron," were equally famous for their devotion to a good cigar. No caricaturist who drew Grant without a cigar in his mouth could hope to rise in his profession. Bismarck once told a group of visitors the following story: "The value of a good cigar," said he, proceeding to light an excellent Havana, "is best understood when it is the last you possess, and there is no chance of getting another. At Königgrätz I had only one cigar left in my pocket, which I carefully guarded during the whole of the battle, as a miser guards his treasure. I did not feel justified in using it. I painted in glowing colors in my mind the happy hour when I should enjoy it after the victory. But I had miscalculated my chances. A poor dragoon lay helpless, with both arms crushed, murmuring for something to refresh him. I felt in my pockets, and found that I had only gold, which would be of no use to him. But stay—I had still my treasured cigar! I lighted it for him, and placed it between his teeth. You should have seen the poor fellow's grateful smile! I never enjoyed a cigar so much as that one which I did not smoke."

THE USES OF CIGAR ASH.

CIGAR ashes, mingled with camphorated chalk, make an excellent tooth-powder; or, ground with poppy-oil, will afford for the use of the painter a varied series of delicate grays. Old Isaac Ostade so utilized the ashes of his pipe, but had he been aware of Havanas, he would have given us pictures even more pearly in tone than those which he has left for the astonishment and delight of mankind.

JULES SANDEAU ON THE CIGAR.

THE cigar is one of the greatest triumphs of the Old World over the New. It would be curious to trace the origin of the cigar, to watch its gradual development, and to observe its rapid growth and wide distribution. We might study, too, all the transformations it has undergone in passing from the homely lips of the commonalty to the rose-colored lips of our dandies. Indeed, its history would not be wholly devoid of interest, for no epoch, perhaps, can show an example of fortune so rapid as that of the cigar. The cigar is ubiquitous ; it is the indispensable complement of all idle and elegant life ; the man who does not smoke cannot be regarded as perfect. The cigar of to-day has taken the place of the little romances, coffee, and verses of the seventeenth century. I am not talking of the primitive cigar, whose poisonous odor and acrid

and repulsive flavor reached one's mar-
tyred lips through the tube of a straw.
Civilization has truly altered such early
simplicity. Spain, Turkey, and Havana
have yielded up to us the most precious
treasures of their smoke-enwrapt dream-
land! and our lips can now filter the perfumed vapor of odoriferous leaves which
have crossed the sea at our summons.
Do not ask me to describe the charms of
the reverie, or the contemplative ecstasy
into which the smoke of our cigar
plunges us. Words are powerless to express or define these "states"; they are
vague and mysterious, as unseizable as
the sweetly scented clouds which are
emitted from your "Mexico" or your
"Panatella." Only let me tell you that
if you have ever found yourself extended
upon a divan with soft and downy
cushions, on some winter's evening, before a clear and sparkling fire, enveloping
the globe of your lamp or the white light
of your wax-candle with the smoke of a

well-seasoned cigar, letting your thoughts
ascend as uncertain and vaporous as the
smoke floating around you, let me tell
you, I repeat, that if you have never yet
enjoyed the situation, you still have to
be initiated into one of the sweetest of
our terrestrial joys. Casanovia, the im-
modest Venetian who wrote his own
memoirs, so that no one should be able
to discover any eccentricities he had not
committed, pretends that the smoker's
sole pleasure consists in seeing the smoke
escape from his lips. I think, O
Venetian! that you have touched a false
note here. The smoke of the cigar produces the same effect as opium, in that
it leads to a state of febrile exaltation, a
perennial source of new pleasures. The
cigar deadens sorrow, distracts our en-
forced inactivity, renders idleness sweet
and easy to us, and peoples our solitude
with a thousand gracious images. Solitude without friend or cigar is indeed in-
supportable to those who suffer. . .

TENNYSON AS A SMOKER.

THE Poet Laureate was a great smoker. He never, with Charles Lamb, praised "Bacchus' black servant, negro fine," nor with Byron hymned the delights of "sublime Tobacco"; but he dearly loved the weed for all that. Poet and dweller in the empyrean though he was, he knew nothing of Mr. Ruskin's scorn for those who "pollute the pure air of the morning with cigar smoke." But he did not affect the Havana in any of its varied forms. His joy was in a pipe of genuine Virginia tobacco. A brother poet, who spent a week with him at his country-seat, says that Partagas, Regalias, and Cabanas had no charm for him.

He preferred a pipe, and of all the pipes in the world the common clay pipe was his choice. His den was at the top of the house. Thither he repaired after breakfast, and in the midst of a sea of books on the shelves, tables, chairs, and floor, toiled away until he was fatigued.

These hours of labor were as absolutely sacred as were Richter's. No human being, unless upon an errand of life or death, was allowed to intrude upon him then ; but when his morning's work was done, he was glad to see his friends—sent for them, indeed, or announced by a little bell his readiness to receive them. As soon as they entered, pipes were lighted. Of these pipes he had a great store, mostly presents from admirers and friends. The visitor had his choice, be it a hookah, narghile, meerschaum, or dhudeen. Tennyson was familiar with all grades of smoking tobacco, and the guest could select at will Latakia, Connecticut leaf, Perique, Lone Jack, Michigan, Killikinick, Highlander, or any of the English brands. The poet himself followed the good old plan of his forefathers, from Raleigh downward. At his feet were a box full of white clay pipes. Filling one of these, he would smoke until it was empty, break it in twain, and throw the fragments into another box prepared for their reception. Then he pulled another pipe from its straw or wooden inclosure, filled it, lighted it, and destroyed it as before. He would not smoke a pipe a second time. Meanwhile, high discourse went on, interrupted not seldom by the poet's reading select passages from the manuscript which was as yet scarcely dry. So the hours were whiled delightfully away until it was time to stroll on the cliffs or dress for dinner.

TOBACCO IN NORTH AMERICA.

MR. FAIRHOLT gives the following version of the Indian tradition as to its first appearance in North America: " A Swedish minister who took occasion to inform the chiefs of the Susquehanna Indians, in a kind of sermon, of the principal historical facts on which the Christian religion is founded, and particularly the fall of our first parents, was thus answered by an old Indian orator: 'What you have told us is very good ; we thank you for coming so far to tell us those things you have heard from your mothers ; in return we will tell you what we have heard from ours. In the beginning we had only flesh of animals to eat ; and if they failed, we starved. Two of our hunters having killed a deer and broiled a part of it, saw a young woman descend from the clouds, and seat herself on a hill hard by. Said one to the other : " It is a spirit, perhaps, that has smelt our venison ; let us offer some of it to her." They accordingly gave her the tongue. She was pleased with its flavor and said : " Your kindness shall be rewarded ; come here thirteen moons hence, and you shall find it." They did so, and found maize growing; where her left hand had been, kidney beans; and where she had sat they found *tobacco.*' "

We are told that the Indians were
so constant in their devotion to the pipe
that they used it as Europeans use a
watch, and in reckoning the time anything occupied would say: " I was one
pipe (of time) about it." When circum-
stances have prevented him from pro-
curing an ordinary pipe, the Indian has
been known to dig a small hole in the
ground, light his tobacco in it, and draw
the smoke through a reed. If they fall
short of provisions when on a long journey, they mix the juice of tobacco with
powdered shells, in the form of little balls,
which they keep in their mouths, and the
gradual solution of which serves to coun-
teract the uneasy craving of the stomach.

SHAKESPEARE AND TOBACCO.

IT is a curious fact that no allusion to " divine Tobacco," as Spenser calls it, is to be found in the works of Shakespeare, though Ben Jonson and his contemporaries indulge in jests at the expense of the lately imported weed, which was smoked under the very noses of the players by the gilded youth of the period, who were wont to take up their positions upon the stage where stools were placed for them, and smoke incessantly during the whole performance.

Shakespeare being the favorite playwright of James I., whose hatred of smoking is well-known, it is not surprising that he failed to notice it favorably in the days of that monarch; but that the companion of Raleigh and Bacon at the " Mermaid " should have nothing to say upon the subject is an enigma which some future Shakespearean scholar may perhaps unravel.

WHAT "TOBACCO" MEANS.

I MUST beg leave to dissent from somebody who has written very unfavorably of smoking tobacco as bad for the lungs, etc. If he means to say that the frequent practice of smoking, and such a habit of doing it as that a man cannot be happy without it, is a prejudicial thing, I agree with him. Tobacco smoke is a stimulant, and therefore the frequent and immoderate use of it must tend to weaken the constitution in the same way, though in a much smaller degree, that dram-drinking or anything else that excites the nervous system does. But against the moderate and occasional use of it there exists no rational objection. It is a valuable article in medicine. I have known much good from its various cases, and have myself been recovered by it, at times, from a languor which neither company nor wine was able to dissipate.

Although, therefore, I shall not decide on the justness of the etymology, I must clearly assent to the truth of the fact asserted by that critic who found its name to be derived from three Hebrew words which, if I recollect aright, were *Tob*-Bonus, *Ach*-Fumus, *A*-Ejus, " Good is the smoke thereof."

—*Gentleman's Magazine* (1788).

EMERSON AND CARLYLE.

THE friendship formed by these two men at Craigenputtock lasted during their lives. There is an unpublished legend to the effect that on the one evening passed at Craigenputtock by Emerson, in 1833, Carlyle gave him a pipe, and, taking one himself, the two sat silent till midnight, and then parted, shaking hands, with congratulations on the profitable and pleasant evening they had enjoyed.

NAPOLEON'S FIRST PIPE.

CONSTANT relates the following anec-
dote of the great NAPOLEON, who once
took a fancy to smoke, for the purpose of
trying a very fine Oriental pipe which
had been presented to him by a Turkish
or Persian ambassador.

"Fire having been brought, it only
remained to communicate it to the tobacco,
but that could never be effected by the
method which his Majesty adopted. He
contented himself with alternately open-
ing and shutting his mouth, without
attempting to draw in his breath. 'Oh,
the devil!' cried he at last, 'there will be
no end of this business.' I observed to
him that he did it half-heartedly, and
showed him how he ought to begin. But
the Emperor always returned to his
yawning. Wearied by his vain efforts, he
at last desired me to light the pipe. I
obeyed, and gave it to him. But scarcely

had he drawn in a mouthful than the smoke, which he knew not how to expel, turned back into his palate, penetrated into his throat, and came out by his nose and blinded him.

"As soon as he recovered his breath, he ejaculated, 'Take that away from me! What abomination! Oh! the swine!— my stomach turns.' In fact, he felt himself so incommoded for at least an hour, that he renounced forever the pleasure of a habit which he said was only fit to amuse sluggards."

MAZZINI'S SANG-FROID AS A SMOKER.

THIS famous Italian exile was forewarned that his assassination had been planned and that men had been dispatched to London for the purpose, but he made no attempt to exclude them from his house. One day the conspirators

entered his room and found him listlessly
smoking. " Take cigars, gentlemen,"
was his instant invitation. Chatting and
hesitation on their part followed. " But
you do not proceed to business, gentle-
men," said Mazzini. " I believe your in-
tention is to kill me." The astounded
miscreants fell on their knees, and at
length departed with the generous par-
don accorded them.

Mazzini's last years in England were
spent at Old Brompton. The modest
chambers he occupied in Onslow Ter-
race were strewed with papers and the
tables provided with cigars, that friends
who called might select their brands and
join him. He always kept a cigar burning
while he wrote. Canaries flew free about
the room. Lord Montairy, in " Lothair,"
smoked cigars so mild and delicate in
flavor that his wife never found him out.
Mazzini surely must have had some Montairy cigars, for his canaries did not find
him out, or object to him if they did!

A SMOKER IN VENICE.

THE late Earl Russell once gave a large party to which the Poet Laureate (Tennyson) was invited, and during the evening his lordship, sauntering up and down his magnificent halls, happened to recognize Tennyson.

"Hau! Mr. Tennyson, how d'ye do? glad to see you. Hau! you've been traveling lately, I hear. How did you like Venice, hau? Fine thing to be in Venice! Did you visit the Bridge of Sighs, hau?"

"Yes."

"And saw all the pictures, hau! and works of art in that wonderful city, did you not, hau?"

"I didn't like Venice!"

"Hau! Indeed! Why not, Mr. Tennyson?"

"They had no good cigars there, my lord; and I left the place in disgust."

MILTON'S PIPE.

MILTON was a smoker. When composing on " Paradise Lost," he portioned out each day in the following manner: As soon as he rose, a chapter of the Bible was read out to him (he was *then* blind). He afterward studied till twelve, taking an hour's exercise before he dined. After dinner, he devoted himself to music, playing on the organ, and he then resumed his studies till six o'clock. Visitors were received from six till eight, at which hour he supped, and having had his pipe of tobacco and glass of water, he retired for the night.

PROFESSOR HUXLEY ON SMOKING.

AT a debate upon " Smoking " among the members of the British Association, many speakers denounced and others advocated the practice. Professor Huxley said, "For forty years of my life, tobacco has been a deadly poison to me. [*Loud cheers from the anti-tobacconists.*] In my youth, as a medical student, I tried to smoke. In vain! at every fresh attempt my insidious foe stretched me prostrate on the floor. [*Repeated cheers.*] I entered the navy; again I tried to smoke, and again met with a defeat. I hated tobacco. I could almost have lent my support to any institution that had for its object the putting of tobacco-smokers to death. [*Vociferous applause.*] A few years ago I was in Brittany with some friends. We went to an inn. They began to smoke. They looked very happy, and outside it was very wet and dismal. I thought I would try a cigar. [*Murmurs.*] I did so. [*Great expectations.*] I smoked that cigar—it was delicious! [*Groans.*] From that moment I was a changed man; and I now feel that smoking in moderation is a comfortable and laudable practice, and is productive of good. [*Dismay and confusion of the anti-tobacconists. Roars of laughter from the smokers.*] There is no more harm in a pipe than there is in a cup of tea. You may poison yourself by drinking too much green tea, and kill yourself by eating too many beef-steaks. For my own part, I consider that tobacco, in moderation, is a sweetener and equalizer of the temper." [*Total rout of the anti-tobacconists and complete triumph of the smokers.*]

ROBERT BURNS' SNUFF-BOX.

ROBERT BURNS was never happier than when he could "pass a winter evening under some venerable roof and smoke a pipe of tobacco or drink water gruel." He also took it in snuff. Mr. Bacon, who kept a celebrated posting-house north of Dumfries, was his almost inseparable associate. Many a merry night did they spend together over their cups of foaming ale or bowls of whisky toddy, and on some of those occasions Burns composed several of his best convivial songs. The bard and the innkeeper became so attached to each other that, as a token of regard, Burns gave Bacon his snuff-box, which for many years had been his pocket companion.

The knowledge of this gift was confined to a few of their jovial brethren. But after Bacon's death, in 1825, when his household furniture was sold by public auction, this snuff-box was offered among other trifles, and someone in the crowd at once bid a shilling for it. There was a general exclamation that it was not worth twopence, and the auctioneer seemed about to knock it down. He first looked, however, at the lid, and then read in a tremendous voice the following inscription upon it: " Robert Burns, officer of the Excise." Scarcely had he uttered the words, says one who was present at the sale, before shilling after shilling was rapidly and confusedly offered for this relic of Scotland's great bard, the greatest anxiety prevailing; while the biddings rose higher and higher, till the trifle was finally knocked down for five pounds. The box was made of the tip of a horn, neatly turned round at the point; its lid is plainly mounted with silver, on which the inscription is engraved.

A SMOKING EMPRESS.

THE Empress of Austria is, perhaps, the only royal or imperial lady of the present age who may be regarded from a nicotian point of view with entire satisfaction. When at home she is generally very tired, and having little taste for reading, lolls back in a deep, soft armchair, or lies on a sofa, puffing cigarettes. She has an album by her, with photographs

of her horses, her favorite dogs, her children, and her grandchild. She hates
brilliant assemblies, and thinks parliaments contemptible. Very capricious
and strong-willed in carrying out her
whims, she can, in the German fashion,
put rank aside, and be very charming to
those who surround her, if such is her
good pleasure. Captain Middleton, who
is her esquire in the hunting-fields of
England and Ireland, has never had a
harsh word from her Majesty. With the
circus-girl Elsie, who was a year or two
ago the idol of the Parisian *boulevardiers*,
her Majesty is almost motherly. The two
smoke cigarettes together, and talk gayly
on equestrian subjects—the only subjects,
indeed, which interest the Kaiserin.

AN INGENIOUS SMOKER.

THE famous Bishop Burnet, like many
authors of later days, was very partial to
tobacco, and always smoked while he was

writing. In order to combine the two
operations with perfect comfort to himself,
he would bore a hole through the broad
brim of his large hat, and putting the
stem of his long pipe through it, puff and
write, and write and puff, with learned
gravity.

This singular device, however, did not
originate with the English divine, since
Heine concludes some ponderous joking
on those who have liked and those who
have disliked tobacco (among the latter
he himself being included), with the re-
mark that the great Boxhornius also loved
tobacco, and that "in smoking he wore a
hat with a broad brim, in the fore part of
which he had a hole, through which the
pipe was stuck, that it might not hinder
his studies."

This famous scholar and critic, who
died at Leyden in 1653, was wont, with
the modesty of genuine erudition, to
say :

"How many things there are that we

do not know!" Whereupon someone has remarked that there was one thing certainly that Boxhornius did not know, and that was how to moderate himself in the use of tobacco, inasmuch as by smoking incessantly he shortened his life.

RALEIGH'S TOBACCO-BOX.

SIR WALTER RALEIGH was no niggard of his tobacco, if we may judge from the size of his box. In 1719 this relic was preserved in the museum of Mr. Ralph Thoresby of Leeds. It was cylindrical in form, about seven inches in diameter and thirteen inches high; the outside was of gilt leather, and in the inside was a cavity for a receiver of glass or metal, which would hold about a pound of tobacco. A kind of collar, connecting the receiver with the case, was pierced with holes for pipes.   , •

SMOKING IN 1610.

FROM the following passage in Ben Jonson's play, "The Alchemist," first acted in 1610, we gather some curious particulars respecting the business of a tobacconist of that period. It occurs in the first act, where *Abel Drugger* is introduced to *Subtle:*

"This my friend Abel, an honest fellow ;
  He lets me have good tobacco, and he does not
  Sophisticate it with sack-lees or oil,
  Nor washes it in muscadel and grains,
  Nor buries it in gravel, underground,
  Wrapped up in greasy leather, . . .
  But keeps it in fine lily pots that, open'd,
  Smell like conserve of roses, or French beans.
  He has his maple block, his silver tongs,
  Winchester pipes, and fire of juniper ;
  A neat, spruce, honest fellow. . ."

The Virginian tobacco was usually imported in the leaf, and had to be rubbed small for smoking. The Spanish tobacco was manufactured into balls about the size of a man's head, and was also imported in the form of what the French term *carottes*, which were known in England by an obscene name, hardly yet obsolete among sailors. Not fifty years ago a story was current in the West Indies, of a facetious reply given by a sailor to his captain's wife, who, happening to see him employed about some tobacco, asked him what he was going to make of it: "*Penem volo fabricari, domina, sed vereor ne ex illo coleos faciam.*" This carotte and ball tobacco was cut as required into small pieces on a maple block with a knife, and the pipe—shorter and straighter in the stem and more upright in the bowl than those of our own day— being filled, was lighted by embers of Juniper wood, taken from a kind of chafing dish by silver tongs.

PIGS AND SMOKERS.

"BROTHER G.," said one clergyman to another, "is it possible you smoke tobacco? Pray, give up the unseemly prac-

tice. It is alike unclerical and uncleanly.
Tobacco! Why, my dear brother, even
a pig would not smoke so vile a weed!"
Brother G. delivered a mild outpouring
of tobacco-fumes, and then as mildly said,
" I suppose, Brother C., you don't smoke?"
" No, indeed!" exclaimed his friend, with
virtuous horror. Another puff or two,
and then Brother G., who prefers the so-
cratic method of argument, rejoined,
" Then, dear brother, which is more like
the pig—you or I?"

THE SOCIAL PIPE.

HONEST men, with pipes or cigars in
their mouths, have great physical advan-
tages in conversation. You may stop
talking if you like, but the breaks of
silence never seem disagreeable, being
filled up by the puffing of the smoke;
hence there is no awkwardness in resum-
ing the conversation, no straining for
effect—sentiments are delivered in a
grave, easy manner. The cigar harmo-

nizes the society, and soothes at once the speaker and the subject whereon he converses. I have no doubt that it is from the habit of smoking that the Turks and American Indians are such monstrous well-bred men. The pipe draws wisdom from the lips of the philosopher, and shuts up the mouth of the foolish ; it generates a style of conversation, contemplative, thoughtful, benevolent and unaffected ; in fact, dear Bob,—I must out with it, —I am an old smoker. At home, I have done it up the chimney rather than not do it (the which I own is a crime).

I vow and believe that the cigar has been one of the greatest creature-comforts of my life—a kind companion, a gentle stimulant, an amiable anodyne, a cementer of friendship.

—THACKERAY.

AGES ATTAINED BY GREAT SMOKERS.

INVETERATE smokers have reached very great ages. Hobbes, who smoked twelve pipes a day at Chatsworth, attained the age of 92; Izaak Walton, 90; Dr. Carr, 78; all devoted lovers of the pipe; and Dr. Isaac Barrow called tobacco his "panpharmacon."

In 1769, died Abraham Favrot, a Swiss baker, aged 104; to the last he walked firmly, read without spectacles, and always had a pipe in his mouth.

In 1845, died Pheasy Molly, of Buxton, Derbyshire, aged 96; she was burned to death, her clothes becoming ignited while lighting her pipe at the fire.

In 1856, there died at Wellbury, North Riding of Yorkshire, Jane Garbutt, aged 110; she retained her faculties and enjoyed her pipe to the last. She had smoked "very nigh a hundred years."

Wadd, in his *Comments on Corpulency*, mentions an aged Effendi, " whose back was bent like a bow, and who was in the habit of taking daily four ounces of rice, thirty cups of coffee, three grains of opium, besides smoking sixty pipes of tobacco." Mr. Chatto, in his amusing *Paper of Tobacco*, relates that some time ago there was living at Hildhausen, in Silesia, a certain Heinrich Hertz, aged 142, who had been a tobacco-taker from his youth and still continued to smoke a pipe or two every day.

Although the lovers of smoking have pressed Old Parr into their evidence in its favor, they must yield to the authority of Taylor, the Water-Poet, who in his *Old, Old, very Old Man ; or, the Age and Life of Thomas Parr*, says :

" He had but little time to waste,
  Or at the ale-house, huff-cap ale to taste ;
  Nor did he ever hunt a tavern fox ;
  Ne'er knew a coach, *tobacco*," etc.

SOME SALESMEN AND OTHERS.

THE typical traveling man knows how to wear good clothes, and will converse upon any subject from protoplasm to the rearing of children. He will " josh " a baby up and down to relieve a tired mother on a long journey, and is willing at any time to usurp from the landscape the pretty girl's attention to himself and his deeds of prowess, from " delightful trips " and " car load lots " to the " best room in the house."

It is not his fault if the pretty girl suffers from *ennui*. If she will only give him a fair show he will surely hit upon something to make her journey pleasant. He knows everybody and everything worth knowing. Her name may be Smith. One of his very best customers— an " elegant gentleman," is named Smith. Or " you remind me very much of a friend in New York." "Never been to New York?" "We will have to look into your case."

And then he draws a very graphic picture "of the only town in the country." She is charmed—nay, fascinated. Perhaps he invites her to have a little lunch on the train. They dine en route, and he owns the car. How the waiter hustles for him. What graceful table manners he affects. What fascinating "nothings" he pours into her ears. Her heart is no longer in the country town. It is traveling at the rate of forty miles an hour and beating very fast. If she were a possible customer now what a bill of goods he would sell. But alas, she is only a trusting maiden. He knows it, and regrets he has charmed her so. He is a gentleman, as most of his kind are. Then he assumes the brotherly rôle, and when her station is reached her heart is back again in the country town. She has a pleasant memory to feed on for some

time to come, and he has had the satisfaction of making what might have been
a tiresome ride a pleasant time for the
maid at least.

Gallant and chivalrous as the " typical "
generally is, he is just as accomplished in
other ways. Versatile to his finger tips,
he is perfectly capable of running the
train (should the conductor suddenly
die) or holding up the passengers, for
that matter, if he found he was
" broke."

But there is a class of traveling men
who possess all of the above qualities, and
some others.

They are the unique creatures who are
known as CIGAR SALESMEN.

" And the wonder of it is there are no
two of them alike."

In fact, there are so many different
kinds of them that if one hundred were
assembled together in one room it would
be impossible to classify them in bunches
of five as " Exhibit A," " B," etc.

There are four distinct types, however, which stand out prominently on the landscape. They are like a certain brand of bicycle—" you see them everywhere," and they don't have to be labeled. For that reason it is easier to draw a pen picture of them.

We will call type No. 1.

Jimmy Smirk to the front. This gentleman is the most beautiful specimen of the cigar salesman now in existence. He was discovered about fifteen years ago—when he was twenty-five years old—sighing and looking at some lavender "pants" in a tailor's window. How he got where he is, is too long a story, but he is at present representing a big cigar manufacturer in the West.

It is said that he is only ten hours behind the latest London and Paris styles. Leading tailors of both these places always have a copy of his route before them so that if any new style is adopted he is cabled to at once. Perhaps this may not be strictly true, but it is given as a fact that last winter he received the following cable from London :

"*Prince of Wales' new overcoat is without pockets.*"

And Jimmy immediately wired back : "*Charming innovation. I'll take the same.*" And so Jimmy was seen once—just once—in Denver, Salt Lake City, San Francisco, and other points with the pocketless overcoat.

Some people thought it a rather giddy coat, and began to make inquiries about the wearer. When they found he was a cigar salesman their admiration was great. Jimmy got into the papers. Smokers began to ask their retail dealer what house he represented. There were so many inquiries, that out of self-protection the retailers had to buy some of Jimmy's cigars. People wanted to know him. They found him a good fellow who knew *how* to wear clothes without being conscious that he was "a man apart."

" Clever dog ! " An advertising genius who makes his luxurious tastes produce sales and profits.

The Cosy Corner cigar salesman couldn't do as Jimmy does. Beware of him. He is as insidious as absinthe. What a rippling, bell-like laugh he has, and stories. It is rumored that he carries a bottle of stuff that when injected into the system produces instantaneous good nature. Clothes ; he'll have none of them that he can't wear all the time. Not even an extra pair of trousers. He sells you a bill of goods when you're not looking. And so easy. You have had the best dinner for many a day, and laughter enough to last a month. " I told that story of yours to fifty people, and they nearly died." In the middle of the second bottle the " Cosy Corner " produces cigars. By that time you love the world. You insist upon giving him a big order. He doesn't want to sell you now, " but, if

you insist, I will book it." That's *his*
way, and you like it.

The cold-blooded business man doesn't
care for small bottles. He never drinks,
and looks upon life through crackers-and-
milk and tea-and-toast spectacles. He
is the closest buyer in the business.
Prices talk with him, and nothing else.
For that reason our friend Charlie
Hustler can do business with him.
Charlie travels for a cheap cigar concern,
sells everybody he can, and when you
turn around to speak to him he is on the
train for the next town. Queer fellow,
Charlie. He is the " Electric Spark " of
the trade. Nobody ever saw him sit
down, or to be without a sample case.
If he is to take a nine o'clock train, you
will find him quoting prices at 8.40 to
some retailer. He carries his cards and
railroad ticket in his hat, makes out his
orders on the train, and foots up his sales
while waiting for the different courses at
dinner. You are wrapt in admiration for

him, but for the real thing the Colonel is the best. Not to know the " Colonel " is to have missed

"A loyal, just, and upright gentleman."

The above quotation is the keynote of the " Colonel's " character, for if there ever was a courteous, chivalrous, and picturesque human being, he is one. Of such stuff as this is the " Colonel " made. Is it any wonder that his success as a cigar salesman has enabled him to retire with all his honors flush upon him.

Ask the " Colonel " to talk about himself and he is silent. " Really, my dear boy, there's nothing interesting about me. It is true I have sold a few cigars in my day, but plenty of others have done the same." From another source, however, you learn that *not* many others have done "the same." You also learn that the " Colonel " is modest, and when you ask him about a twenty-five thousand dollar sale he once made, he does admit it was true.

" What was your secret in selling cigars ? "

" Simply doing the best I know how. Telling the truth about my goods, so that the customer knew it was the truth, and letting the price do the rest."

And there you have the " Colonel." There was no secret in his way of doing business, and since he will not talk about himself, let us hear what he has to say in a general way.

" A large dry goods merchant out in Chicago used to say to his traveling men : ' Keep down your expenses. Remember that a cigar goes a long way.'

" This may or may not be true in the dry goods business," continued the " Colonel."   " In the cigar trade the giving of a cigar cuts no figure.   It could not by any possible means bring about a friendly feeling between buyer and salesman. If the cigar is good, and your prices right, it will assist, like a sample of anything else, to make the sale. Cigars given away socially should go a long way, however.

" To me it is a proof of esteem to have a friend give me one of his cigars. Something that he has put time, trouble, and even study in finding to his taste, he shares with me. Isn't that a graceful compliment to pay a friend ?

" While on the subject, did you ever think that a profitable school of instruction for salesmen could be started? There's a great field here for some ex-traveling salesmen to use his past experience profitably.

" Take dealing with buyers, for instance ; what a course of study that calls for alone ! Of course there can be no instruction that will teach a salesman how to successfully approach every buyer, but there are a few principles and laws which every salesman ought to know, but doesn't. For example, I believe that after the salesman has announced the name of the firm he travels for, he should, without being officious, be sure that the buyer knows his own name. Quite a little important point, and one which is frequently overlooked.

"After a man has been traveling for some time, he will find out that buyers are only human beings after all. You have *got* to be a diplomat to succeed as a salesman. Five minutes' talk with a buyer ought to be enough. Then size him up and proceed cautiously. How often has a good story helped to sell a bill of goods! How often a word too much or too little has killed a sale! How often has the knowledge (discreetly used) of a buyer's 'pet hobby' been the only means of making a sale!

"To sum it all up, to be a successful salesman you've got to be prepared to take an interest in everything on earth. In other words, as a newspaper man says of his vocation, to be 'newborn every day.'

" Some good writer will make a hit one of these days with a series of cigar character sketches, making the cigars tell the story of their life and adventures. For instance, what a story a tenement-house cigar could tell ! The people it has associated with from start to finish, and its vicissitudes. You can easily see there's a wealth of literary material here.

" I remember very well the first tenement-house cigars which were put on the market. The salesmen were nothing but peddlers. They went out on the road with their stock of cigars, and, like the fish peddlers, didn't come home until they had sold out.

" Salesmen for the tenement-house concerns were versatile characters in the early days. They had to be. A friend of mine who travels for one of these houses was suddenly wired to come home when he was doing a good business. He couldn't understand it until he arrived at the factory. He found a red-hot strike in progress and an excited lot of cigarmakers outside the building about to break in the door and attack those working inside. Climbing through a back window he grabbed a piece of lead pipe and guarded the door just as the strikers were about to force it open. It wasn't exactly a 'lead pipe cinch' for him, but he stood his ground until his employers had a chance to go for the police.

"When they arrived on the scene his work was over, and he walked right out among the crowd of strikers, boarded a train out of town, and the next day was selling cigars as if nothing had happened.

"About the worst cigars are made in Pennsylvania by the farmers and their families during the winter. The tobacco is of course grown on their own land, and they make a good living by filling in the winter months making these fire-brands. They are sold to all sorts of strange people and fakirs, and are often known as 'scheme cigars'; that is, they are sold with clocks, cheap watches, and pictures.

" A strong, muscular traveling man who represented one of these scheme-cigar concerns, told me not long ago that he is physically unable to smoke his own samples. He wipes out a good many quiet old grudges with these cigars during a year.

" Historical names are to my mind by far the best to give cigars. They recall so much and linger with you when other names are forgotten. There's the flavor of romance about them. Your favorite heroes are carried back to your boyhood schooldays with pleasant memories, and in spite of yourself when you go to buy a cigar, some historical name is on the tip of your tongue.

" In spite of the fact that the cigar trade is just as cold-blooded as any other when it comes to doing business, still no one can deny that in the poorest and meanest cigar, there is, or ought to be, a certain sentiment which is not associated with any other manufactured article. From the green fields of tobacco to the cigar in a box surrounded by bright labels and ribbons, it is always a picturesque creation. There is nothing that will take its place on this earth. And since that is so, let me offer you one of my special brand."

The "Colonel" lit his cigar and the writer joined him. After a few puffs, he said, "Nothing else in the world except a cigar could put an end to my rambling remarks." In a few minutes he was lost in a cloud, and the interview ended.

PUFFS.

ABOUT four and a quarter billion cigars were manufactured in this country last year, and the government got the "rake off"—over twelve million dollars.

TOBACCO in any form is good for the teeth. (Please don't dispute this.) This doesn't mean that it takes the place of a tooth brush. That's a different proportion altogether, as they say in Colorado.

THE famous *Vuelta Abajo* district will not be very much in evidence next year as far as producing tobacco is concerned. Already at this writing the '96 crop is only one-tenth of what it usually is, and the tobacco garden of Cuba has been devastated to a condition of sadness which nothing except war could accomplish.
But while this portion of the island is only waiting to be permitted to breathe a

little new life, it is still the same soil and climate. And nowhere else on "God's green acres" grows a plant equal in fragrance and aroma to the tobacco raised in the Vuelta Abajo (" The Lower Turn ") district. It is the Sunset Land of Cuba—the tail of the island—not un- like the shape of an alligator. It is in the province of *Pinar del Rio*—" The Pine of the River "—about 150 miles long and 40 wide, the tobacco growing portion being only one-half of the province in length and width.

It is a diversified country. Here a sea- coast, there a forest, now a series of rocky hills skirted by a valley of flat lands where grows the beautiful plant.

HE who smokes and lays away,
Will smoke the same another day.

MME. HELENA MODJESKA, one of the most charming of women and certainly an actress, if there ever was one, smokes cigarettes. And there are people who

say that no lady will ever smoke a cigarette. According to that no gentleman
will smoke a cigar, much less a pipe.

And yet we have smoked with some
very gentle-men.

A cigar is a cigar for a' that.

MOST men of talent and genius use or
have used tobacco in some form. Those
who don't, while they are none the less
great, are surely less happy. What a
round of reveries and delightful musings
they have missed! Napoleon, for instance, if he had only learned to smoke,
might have made a better record for himself, certainly a more humane one, and
his days of St. Helena would have been
so calm, peaceful, and reflective that he
would have given us a study of the times
(had he smoked) that would now be
among the classics of literature.

Look at the " big smokers " of to-day,
and outside of their greatness what
" good fellows " they are. Here are

some of them—Thomas A. Edison, Sir Henry Irving, Buffalo Bill, Bismarck, Prince of Wales, Marion Crawford, Richard Mansfield, Colonel Ingersoll, Henry George, Henry Watterson, James Gordon Bennett, Frank Work, Carl Schurz, Speaker Reed, Francis Wilson, De Wolf Hopper, and lots of others.

A CRITIC once discovered that the great difference between two celebrated French painters, Décamps and Horace Vernet, was mainly the effect of their habits as users of tobacco. The French Murillo, the Oriental colorist, the sublime Décamps, smoked a pipe. Vernet toyed with the cigarette.

ON A BROKEN PIPE.

NEGLECTED now it lies, a cold clay form,
So late with living inspirations warm ;
Type of all other creatures formed of
    clay,
What more than it for epitaph have
    they ?

TOBACCO, some say, is a potent narcotic,
That rules half the world in a way quite
    despotic ;
So to punish him well for his wicked and
    merry tricks,
We'll burn him forthwith, as they used
    to do heretics.

A GOOD name for a cigar is at any time
worth one hundred dollars per letter.
There is no other trade that uses or possi-
bly can use so many titles for its wares.
The thousands of beautiful names given
to cigars show that cigar manufacturers
are a very appreciative lot of people, and
are quite as much (if not more) advanced
in the philosophy and poetry of life as any
other class of business men.

A glance at the registrations of cigar
names will verify the above at any time.
There is scarcely a name of history,
romance, and song which could be used
in good taste but what is used on the
cover of a cigar box. A young man who

thought he had a "good thing" recently
submitted one hundred names to the
Tobacco Leaf. He found all but four
of them had been used, and he went sadly
away, leaving the names behind.

I OWE to smoking, more or less,
Through life the whole of my success;
With my cigar I'm sage and wise,
Without, I'm dull as cloudy skies.
When smoking, all my ideas soar,
When not they sink upon the floor.
The greatest men have all been smokers,
And so were all the greatest jokers.
Then ye who'd bid adieu to care
Come here and smoke it into air.

J. DYER BALL, ESQ., in his book
"Things Chinese," says concerning pipe
(tobacco) smoking in China : "There are
two kinds of pipes in use: the dry pipe and
the water pipe. The latter is a copy of the
Indian hookah ; it consists of a receptacle

for the water into which a tube-like piece, about the size of a small finger, is inserted ; the upper end of this tube contains a small cavity into which the tobacco is put. The smoke is inhaled through the water up the pipe part, which is a tube about a foot long gradually narrowing and bending over at the mouthpiece. These pipes are made of an alloy of copper, zinc, nickel, and sometimes a little silver, and are used by ladies and gentlemen.

" The other pipes are often made of bamboo, as far as the stems are concerned, and vary in length from a few feet to a few inches. The bowls, of metal, are small, holding scarcely more than a thimbleful of tobacco ; a few whiffs exhaust them, and, with the gentleman or lady, a servant is ready who steps up, takes the pipe, empties out the ashes, refills it, sticks it into the mouth of his master or mistress, and lights it with a paper spill."

IN the Quartier Latin of Paris the pipe has ever been the great consoler in the bachelor homes of Bohemian artists, and has ever usurped the sway of women, as in the case of the artist Gavarni, who on his deathbed is reported to have said to a friend: " I leave you my wife and my pipe ; take care of my pipe."

NATIONAL CHARACTERISTICS.

AN Englishman and a Frenchman were traveling together in a diligence, and both smoking. Monsieur did all in his power to draw his phlegmatic fellow-passenger into conversation, but to no purpose. At last, with a superabundance of politeness, he apologized for drawing his attention to the fact that the ash of his cigar had fallen on his waistcoat, and that a spark was endangering his neck-erchief.

The Englishman, now thoroughly aroused, exclaimed : " Why the devil can't you let me alone! Your coat-tail has been on fire for the last ten minutes, but I didn't bother you about it!"

TOBACCO AND THE PLAGUE.

WHILE the Great Plague raged in London, tobacco was recommended by the faculty, and generally taken as a preventive against infection. Pepys records the following on the 7th of June, 1665: " The hottest day that ever I felt in my life. This day, much against my will, I did in Drury Lane see two or three houses marked with a red cross upon the doors, and 'Lord, have mercy upon us!' writ there ; which was a sad sight to me, being the first of the kind, to my remembrance, I ever saw. It put me into an ill conception of myself and my smell, so that I was forced to buy some roll tobacco to smell and chew, which took away the apprehension."

Further, it was popularly reported that no tobacconists or their households were afflicted by the plague. Physicians who visited the sick took it very freely; the men who went round with the dead carts had their pipes continually alight. This gave tobacco a new popularity, and it again took the high medical position accorded to it by the physicians of the French Court.

IF a cigar kills you it's bad.

LET him now smoke who never smoked before,
And he who always smoked now smoke the more.

 Trieste

Trieste Publishing has a massive catalogue of classic book titles. Our aim is to provide readers with the highest quality reproductions of fiction and non-fiction literature that has stood the test of time. The many thousands of books in our collection have been sourced from libraries and private collections around the world.

The titles that Trieste Publishing has chosen to be part of the collection have been scanned to simulate the original. Our readers see the books the same way that their first readers did decades or a hundred or more years ago. Books from that period are often spoiled by imperfections that did not exist in the original. Imperfections could be in the form of blurred text, photographs, or missing pages. It is highly unlikely that this would occur with one of our books. Our extensive quality control ensures that the readers of Trieste Publishing's books will be delighted with their purchase. Our staff has thoroughly reviewed every page of all the books in the collection, repairing, or if necessary, rejecting titles that are not of the highest quality. This process ensures that the reader of one of Trieste Publishing's titles receives a volume that faithfully reproduces the original, and to the maximum degree possible, gives them the experience of owning the original work.

We pride ourselves on not only creating a pathway to an extensive reservoir of books of the finest quality, but also providing value to every one of our readers. Generally, Trieste books are purchased singly - on demand, however they may also be purchased in bulk. Readers interested in bulk purchases are invited to contact us directly to enquire about our tailored bulk rates. Email: customerservice@triestepublishing.com

You May Also Like

ISBN: 9781760573447
Paperback: 290 pages
Dimensions: 6.0 x 0.61 x 9.0 inches
Language: eng

"Ladies from Hell". Illustrated with Photographs

R. Douglas Pinkerton

ISBN: 9780649059638
Paperback: 126 pages
Dimensions: 6.14 x 0.27 x 9.21 inches
Language: eng

A Place of Repentance; Or, an Account of the London Colonial Training Institution and Ragged Dormitiry, for the Reformation of Youthful and Adult Male Criminals, Great Smith Street, Westminster

Samuel Martin

www.triestepublishing.com

You May Also Like

Speed Control of Induction Motors for Rolling Mill Service; Bachelor's Thesis

Jerome Henry Gefke

ISBN: 9780649070558
Paperback: 140 pages
Dimensions: 6.14 x 0.30 x 9.21 inches
Language: eng

Florentine Notes

Henry Greenough Huntington

ISBN: 9781760579791
Paperback: 118 pages
Dimensions: 6.14 x 0.25 x 9.21 inches
Language: eng

www.triestepublishing.com

You May Also Like

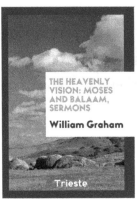

The heavenly vision: Moses and Balaam, sermons

Unknown

ISBN: 9780649295418
Paperback: 68 pages
Dimensions: 5.83 x 0.14 x 8.27 inches
Language: eng

The Just Supremacy of Congress Over the Territories

Unknown

ISBN: 9780649244690
Paperback: 50 pages
Dimensions: 6.14 x 0.10 x 9.21 inches
Language: eng

You May Also Like

ISBN: 9780649371006
Paperback: 94 pages
Dimensions: 6.14 x 0.19 x 9.21 inches
Language: eng

Theosophical Manuals I
elementary theosophy

Unknown

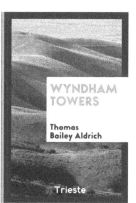

ISBN: 9780649335374
Paperback: 86 pages
Dimensions: 6.14 x 0.18 x 9.21 inches
Language: eng

Wyndham Towers

Unknown

Find more of our titles on our website. We have a selection of thousands of titles that will interest you. Please visit

www.triestepublishing.com

Lightning Source UK Ltd.
Milton Keynes UK
UKHW02f2018130618
324198UK00004B/405/P